GLOBAL ISSUES

Series editors: Stephen Hay

*H*EALING FOR *B*ROKEN *P*EOPLE

Dan
Harrison

with Maria Henderson

**6 Studies
for individuals
or groups**

INTERVARSITY PRESS
DOWNERS GROVE, ILLINOIS 60515

12	11	10	9	8	7	6	5	4	3	2	1
99	98	97	96	95	94	93	92	91	90		

Contents

Because humankind is made in the image of God, every person, regardless of race, religion, color, culture, class, sex or age, has an intrinsic dignity because of which he or she should be respected and served, not exploited. Here too we express penitence both for our neglect and for having sometimes regarded evangelism and social concern as mutually exclusive.

Although reconciliation with people is not reconciliation with God, nor is social action evangelism, nor is political liberation salvation, nevertheless we affirm that evangelism and sociopolitical involvement are both part of our Christian duty. For both are necessary expressions of our doctrines of God and humankind, our love for our neighbor and our obedience to Jesus Christ.

The message of salvation implies also a message of judgment upon every form of alienation, oppression and discrimination, and we should not be afraid to denounce evil and injustice wherever they exist.

—*Lausanne Covenant, Article Five.*

Welcome to Global Issues Bible Studies

With all the rapid and dramatic changes happening in our world today, it's easy to be overwhelmed and simply withdraw. But it need not be so for Christians! God has not only given us the mandate to love the world, he has given us the Holy Spirit and the community of fellowship to guide us and equip us in the ministry of love.

Ministering in the world can be threatening: It requires change in both our lifestyle and our thinking. We end up discovering that we need to cling closer to Jesus than ever before—and that becomes the great personal benefit of change. God's love for the world is the same deep love he has for you and me.

This study series is designed to help us understand what is going on in *the world*. Then it takes us to *the Word* to help us be faithful in our compassionate response. The series is firmly rooted in the evangelical tradition which calls for a personal saving relationship with Jesus Christ and a public lifestyle of discipleship that demonstrates the Word has truly come alive in us.

At the front of the guide is an excerpt from the Lausanne Covenant which we have found helpful. We have developed this series in keeping with the spirit of the covenant, especially sections four and five. You may wish to refer to the Lausanne Covenant for further guidance as you form your own theology of evangelism and social concern.

In the words of the covenant's authors we challenge you: "The salvation we claim should be transforming us in the totality of our personal and social responsibilities. Faith without works is dead."

Getting the Most from Global Issues Bible Studies

Global Issues Bible Studies are designed to be an exciting and challenging way to help us seek God's will for all of the world as it is found in Scripture. As we learn more about the world, we will learn more about ourselves as well.

How They Are Designed

Global Issues Bible Studies have a number of distinctive features. First, each guide has an introduction from the author which will help orient us to the significant questions which the studies will deal with.

Second, the Bible study portion is inductive rather than deductive. The author will lead us to discover what the Bible says about a particular topic through a series of questions rather than simply telling us what he or she believes. Therefore, the studies are thought-provoking. They help us to think about the meaning of the passage so that we can truly understand what the biblical writer intended to say.

Third, the studies are personal. Global Issues Bible Studies are not just theoretical studies to be considered in private or discussed in a group. These studies will motivate us to action. They will expose us to the promises, assurances, exhortations and challenges of God's Word. Through the study of Scripture, we will renew our minds so that we can be transformed by the Spirit of God.

Fourth, the guides include resource sections that will help you to act on the challenges Scripture has presented you with.

Fifth, these studies are versatile. They are designed for student, mission, neighborhood and/or church groups. They are also effective for individual study.

How They Are Put Together

Global Issues Bible Studies also have a distinctive format. Each study need take no more than forty-five minutes in a group setting or thirty minutes in personal study—unless you choose to take more time.

Each guide has six studies. If the guides are used in pairs, they can be used within a quarter system in a church and fit well in a semester or trimester system on a college campus.

The guides have a workbook format with space for writing responses. This is ideal for personal study and lets group members prepare in advance for the discussion. In addition the last question in each study offers suggestions and opportunity for personal response.

At the end of the guides are some notes for leaders. They describe how to lead a group discussion, give helpful tips on group dynamics and suggest ways to deal with problems which may arise during the discussion. With such helps, someone with little or no experience can lead an effective study.

Suggestions for Individual Study

1. As you begin, pray that God will help you understand and apply the passages to your life. Pray that he will show you what kinds of action he would have you take as a result of your time of study.

2. In your first session take time to read the introduction to the entire guide. This will orient you to the subject at hand and the author's goals for the studies.

3. Read the short introduction to the study.

4. Read and reread the suggested Bible passages to familiarize yourself with them.

5. A good modern translation of the Bible, rather than the King James Version or a paraphrase, will give you the most help. The New International Version, the New American Standard Bible and the Revised Standard Version are all recommended. The questions in this guide are based on the New International Version.

6. Use the space provided to respond to the questions. This will help you express your understanding of the passage clearly.

7. Look up the passages listed under *For Further Study* at the end of each study. This will help you to better understand the principles outlined in the main passages and give you an idea of how these

themes are found throughout Scripture.

8. It might be good to have a Bible dictionary handy. Use it to look up any unfamiliar words, names or places.

9. Take time with the final question in each study to commit yourself to action and/or a change in attitude.

Suggestions for Group Study

1. Come to the study prepared. Follow the suggestions for individual study mentioned above. You will find that careful preparation will greatly enrich your time spent in group discussion.

2. Be willing to participate in the discussion. The leader of your group will not be lecturing. Instead, he or she will be encouraging the members of the group to discuss what they have learned. The leader will be asking the questions that are found in this guide.

3. Stick to the topic being discussed. Your answers should be based on the verses which are the focus of the discussion and not on outside authorities such as commentaries or speakers.

4. Be sensitive to the other members of the group. Listen attentively when they describe what they have learned. You may be surprised by their insights! When possible, link what you say to the comments of others. Also, be affirming whenever you can. This will encourage some of the more hesitant members of the group to participate.

5. Be careful not to dominate the discussion. We are sometimes so eager to express our thoughts that we leave too little opportunity for others to respond. By all means participate! But allow others to also.

6. Expect God to teach you through the passage being discussed and through the group. Pray that you will have an enjoyable and profitable time together, but also that as a result of the study, you will find ways that you can take action individually and/or as a group.

7. If you are the discussion leader, you will find additional suggestions at the back of the guide.

God bless you in your adventure of love.

Steve Hayner and Gordon Aeschliman

Introducing Healing for Broken People

"Boy, are you going to get into big trouble! And when you do, don't call on me."

That was my father's reaction to my pride and joy—a 1949 Ford that I had bought against his wishes. I had earned the money to buy that car, and I was determined to drive it. However, I was fifteen and didn't have a driver's license, so I had conned my girlfriend's father into licensing it for me.

I was driving through the city of Ithaca one day when I saw the police car behind me. I pulled over. The next thing I knew I was in jail. My sentence for driving without a license was fifty dollars or thirty days in jail. I didn't have fifty dollars, so I called my dad. If there was any time in my life I thought I needed my dad, it was then. True to his word, he refused to talk to me. He wouldn't even let my mother help me—she was a soft touch, and I knew I could get her to bail me out. Eventually some friends pitched in and got me out, but the anger and rage I felt toward my father was nearly overwhelming.

Understanding Dysfunctionality

When I gave my life to the Lord Jesus several years later, I thought that he would take care of my problems. I was disappointed when I learned that my lifelong struggle with anger was still very much with me. My relationship with my father was restored through God's grace over a period of three years just before he died, but anger continued to spill out in other areas of my life—in my marriage, my relationships with my children, my ministry.

I don't have as many problems with anger now as I did as a teen, but I've come to see that anger is just one area of weakness rooted in my childhood experience of growing up in a dysfunctional family. I've also seen God teach me to grow through these weaknesses and his faithfulness to turn weakness into strength.

Dysfunctional families have been around since Cain killed Abel. But what do we really mean by the term, and how can we describe the children who come out of these families? Dysfunctional families are sometimes defined by characteristics such as divorce, an alcoholic or otherwise addicted parent, or the presence of physical or sexual abuse. My family was not like that at all, but it was still dysfunctional.

My parents were missionaries who served in China among Tibetans for twenty-three years. They took seriously the command to "seek first the kingdom of God" and trusted God to take care of their children. Yet when I look at the family dynamics that mark dysfunctional families, I recognize many of the realities of my home situation.

Dysfunctional families tend to be characterized by a set of rigid, inhumane rules, while functional families have rules that are flexible and designed to meet the needs of the members of the family. In dysfunctional families communication is indirect: Feelings are not expressed openly; certain subjects are never discussed (a parent's drinking problem, for instance); and conflict is avoided at all costs. In functional families, members communicate openly and directly, and they work out their differences in an atmosphere of love and acceptance.

Children in functional families see themselves as loved and respected members of the family. Dysfunctional families give children distorted images of themselves: implicitly blaming the child for family problems, denying the child's worth through abuse, or simply ignoring the child's need for love and nurture. Children in functional families feel secure and valued for themselves. Children in dysfunctional families experience insecurity and find it difficult to trust people.

Defining Codependence

In recent years family therapists and professionals working in the field of chemical dependency have begun to discover similarities among people who grew up in dysfunctional families of all types. Increasingly, the term *codependent* is being used to describe the adults who grew up in these families.

The term arose when psychologists treating alcoholics began to look at the role played by spouses and children. They concluded that the spouse who nagged or covered up for an alcoholic partner was in some sense participating in the addiction. They also realized that even when the alcoholic became sober, other members of the family frequently felt that things had gotten worse. Building on this insight, therapists began to treat codependence in ways paralleling the treatment of alcoholism and other addictions.

The growing numbers of people who identify with the characteristics of codependence provide evidence of the unhealthy nature of many families in our society. Since the early 1980s there have been more than one million divorces each year, with at least a million children affected. Around twelve million people in the United States are alcoholics, each one of them having a negative impact on four or more people around them, including an estimated fifteen million children. Nearly half of those who grow up with an alcoholic parent will eventually marry an alcoholic themselves. By the age of sixteen, one out of four girls has been sexually abused. Eating disorders afflict sixty per cent of the women in America and fifty per cent of the men. The number of single-parent families has grown by fifty per cent since 1970; more and more of these families are headed by women living below the poverty line, so that the stress and potential for dysfunction are increased. Violence is a characteristic of some fifteen million families.

While these statistics indicate an increasing number of people at risk of growing up in a dysfunctional environment, there are some theorists in the field who claim that codependence applies to one degree or another to nearly everyone in our society: it is a cultural syndrome and part of our society's generally addictive approach to life.

Codependence is generally described by a series of characteristics or symptoms, some or all of which might apply to any one person. Many of these symptoms can be manifested as one extreme or another. For example, codependents can be extremely irresponsible or hyper-responsible. We can be total conformists or utter rebels. We can be high achievers or dropouts from society. We can be extremely quiet, unemotional types or explosively angry people. We can seem self-assured to the point of arrogance or self-effacing to the point of invisibility.

Children learn from what they experience, and their amazing powers of adaptation can help them survive unbelievable situations. Adult codependence often arises from coping mechanisms developed in childhood—mechanisms that have become deeply ingrained, but no longer work. Instead of helping the person to cope, they backfire and multiply problems and stress in adulthood.

The following codependent symptoms encompass many of the key tendencies:

Codependents find it extremely difficult to deal with feelings in a healthy way. We may express them explosively, hold them in, be unaware of them or be unable to feel at all. Anger is a major issue for codependents, one that surfaces on several different levels. On one level, codependents have much to be angry about. Codependents have often been victims of abuse or in some way deprived of their childhood. We continue to make ourselves victims in current relationships by being overly dependent.

The problem with anger for a codependent is that, as with any other emotion, he or she does not know how to deal with it in mature, healthy ways. Most codependents grew up in environments that taught them that the best thing to do with feelings—especially "negative" ones like anger—is to act as if one is not feeling them. Pretending that emotions don't exist is like walking across a busy street and pretending that bus isn't coming: you can succeed one hundred per cent in convincing yourself that there is no bus, but it will still hit you if you walk in front of it.

Emotions are energy; they eventually get expressed, one way or another. Anger turned inward is a deadly force, leading to physical symptoms like ulcers or emotional ones like depression. Anger also breeds resentment and bitterness which slowly but surely dominate our characters and turn us into sour, negative people. And even when we have done our best to stuff our anger under the rug, it tends to slip out the sides, manifesting itself in sarcasm and other "unintentionally" harmful behavior.

Then there are codependents who have learned to use anger as a shield. People walk around us on tiptoes, afraid of setting off a torrent of angry words. They have no idea what action or comment might touch a point of insecurity and set off the big guns. This kind of use of anger is abusive to others and keeps others from getting too close.

Codependents tend to be controllers. We attempt to control ourselves, circumstances and other people, often through manipulation and deception. Codependents frequently are motivated by a need to take care of people close to them, usually in a way that suffocates the person and creates an angry backlash.

Underneath this controlling behavior lies a problem that psychologists call *weak boundaries*. The term refers to an underdeveloped sense of the difference between you and me. Codependents feel responsible for other people's thoughts, feelings and actions. We worry obsessively about other people and their problems. Sometimes we find it hard to recognize that we are not responsible for what someone else is feeling—and we let ourselves feel guilty about the prospect of disappointing someone. People-pleasing is a common trait of codependents, and it has its roots in this urge to make sure everyone else around us is feeling OK, even if we are not.

As much as codependents find themselves driven by what they perceive to be other people's desires, they are also expert manipulators. We know how things are "supposed to be," and so we badger, criticize and manipulate others into conforming to our view of the universe. Guilt is usually the medium of exchange for these transactions: if we succeed in making the other person feel guilty, he or she will usually do what we want.

This is false guilt; we might call it "unearned guilt." It has nothing to do with what we feel when we have sinned or violated our own values. That kind of guilt leads to repentance and forgiveness, but false guilt is a prison where we give people power to control us and similarly attempt to control others.

Codependents also have problems with self-esteem. We find it difficult to accept our own worth, independent of what we do or what others think of us. Perfectionism and workaholism are common traits that usually stem from lack of healthy self-esteem. We are constantly trying to prove our worth by doing more things, better and faster than others. We *feel* indispensable—no one else is quite as capable as we are—and sometimes we succeed in convincing others that we *are* indispensable. Codependents are often in the position of trying to work harder to make up for some perceived weakness. Insecurity drives an engine that sooner or later runs out of control.

For a perfectionist, everything is either a total, unqualified success or an abject failure. With such a fragile sense of one's own self-worth, failure is a thing to be avoided at all costs. Yet inevitably the perfectionist maneuvers himself or herself into a place where failure is inevitable because the task is simply too great.

Perfectionism is also linked to the fact that codependents generally come from homes where there was a rigid set of rules. The way to stay out of trouble in such a home was to adhere to the rules—if we could just obey them perfectly, we would have no more problems. In adulthood, the perfectionist thinks that breaking the rules or not living up to unreasonable expectations will result in disaster all out of proportion to the situation. This is another example of the kind of distorted thinking that is often part of codependence.

Focusing on causes and effects and seeing those causes in an essentially self-centered way leads to all kinds of faulty conclusions. The wife of an alcoholic might think that if she keeps the house perfectly clean, her husband will quit drinking. She cannot see that those things are not really related at all.

Another major trait of codependence is denial. *Codependents have a hard time accepting reality*—from the inner reality of our own emotions to the fact that we cannot control everything and everyone we come in contact with. We spend a great deal of energy hiding reality from ourselves and others. We deny our pain. We deny the nature of our problems. We deny ourselves. We accept lies as truth— whether they come from an addicted loved one or from our own twisted thinking—and truth becomes devalued, something to be feared instead of a source of freedom. Denial means that one is not free; as one author on codependence has written, "An addiction is anything we feel we have to lie about."[1] Codependents are in bondage to something that is sucking the life out of them.

As codependence progresses, lethargy, depression and even suicidal tendencies can appear, as well as serious physical and mental illness. Codependents are trying to do the impossible: keep the world, themselves and those they love under control. Eventually the strain of trying to play God wears them out. If indeed it is a disease, it is a potentially fatal one: statistics indicate that alcoholics have a higher life expectancy than their spouses.

Healing for Codependence

Those writing about codependence today, who invariably identify themselves as codependents, generally point toward one path of recovery: the Twelve Steps of Alcoholics Anonymous. These steps have been adapted to help people deal with many addictive and compulsive behaviors. They emphasize that the solution to codependence is spiritual. The Twelve Steps offer an approach to life based on daily dependence on God for the strength to overcome addiction or codependence (see the appendix for a complete list of the steps).

I have worked through a Twelve-Step Program, and my ongoing recovery has been the evidence of God's work in my life over the past twenty-five or thirty years. I have been aware of the notion of dysfunctional families only in the past few years, and the ideas related to codependence are even more recent, yet God has used various people and experiences in my life to work through these issues, and in turn he has used me and my story to encourage others.

One very important experience happened at the beginning of our second mission term in Papua New Guinea, where I was headmaster of the high school for missionary children. I found myself being extremely critical of everyone around me. I would sit in the back of the church and see the backs of my colleagues' heads (almost everyone there was a fellow missionary) and mentally critique them. I was hard on the school's teachers and students alike. I was especially critical of my family. Out of my own insecurity, I found myself picking on my wife, Shelby, constantly trying to make her into some ideal I had in my mind.

Around that time another missionary couple shared with us their experience of praying for God to heal the memories of their adopted son who regularly woke up with terrible nightmares. Shelby and I invited them to pray for us. I saw the difference in my attitude the next Sunday when a friend of mine was preaching. He was simply reading his sermon manuscript, which is something I would normally criticize. Instead, I recall sitting in the back of the church and, rather than thinking critically about the people I saw, rejoicing over them and praying for them.

My bad memories were not gone, but the pain and insecurity that had resulted from those incidents were healed. Gradually, I found myself more accepting and less critical in other situations. I found myself more secure and less willing to criticize Shelby.

Another important lesson had to do with forgiveness. During our first missionary furlough, some friends persuaded us to attend a Basic Youth Conflicts Seminar. Out of a weekend of teaching, the one thing that gripped my heart was Bill Gothard's teaching on forgiveness and the responsibility of Christians to reconcile relationships. I came away knowing that I had to seek forgiveness from each of my siblings and some of their spouses.

I didn't want to do it at all. I had been offended by my brothers and sister. I felt they were responsible to make it right with me. But I knew I had to and began to take steps to meet with each of them. In the process I had to forgive them too. I did talk to my siblings, and in each case there were tears and hugs, acceptance and forgiveness. It was a healing experience for me and the start of a new way of thinking and living that has been a key to recovery for me.

Recently one of my peers erupted in the middle of a meeting, accused me of all sorts of things, and said that he'd been losing sleep over my failings. My immediate response was to be angry and hurt. I felt that his outburst was out of proportion to reality. Just as I was about to start explaining myself, the Lord helped me to see the experience from his perspective and feel some of what he was feeling, and I recognized that I was in some way responsible for that hurt.

I said to him: "I feel awful that you lost sleep over this. I want to ask your forgiveness for being insensitive to your feelings and not investing the time to explain what I was doing and why." He was totally disarmed. A potentially divisive situation within our ministry team was averted, and we could work out our problem peacefully.

Our family has developed a tradition of affirmation in which we go around the table after a special family dinner and tell each person what we appreciate about him or her. It is one of the ways we have discovered to do what Paul instructs the Philippians to do: "Whatever is true, whatever is noble, whatever is right, whatever is pure, whatever is lovely, whatever is admirable—if anything is excellent or praiseworthy—think about such things" (Phil 4:8).

At one point not too many years ago, I suffered a major setback. I was in a working relationship in which I was trying hard to be faithful in applying the things God had taught me, but nothing was working. I felt a total failure. I was as low as I had ever been in my life. In fact, I was so depressed that I didn't even trust myself to drive across town to a doctor's appointment. So Shelby drove me. As soon as we got in the car, she said, "Pull out a piece of paper. I want you to write down something you like about yourself."

I couldn't come up with anything. I could not think of any realm of my life in which I felt useful or had done something worthwhile.

So Shelby started to come up with some things, and told me to write them down: "I am an excellent husband." "I am a child of the King." "I am a great lover." At first I didn't believe those things. Then she had me read the list out loud. I felt as if she were my mother telling me to eat my peas, but it was what I needed. By the time we reached the doctor's, I was feeling almost human again.

In our family we call this "remembering the givens." The givens are the truths of our faith and our experience of one another that form the basis of our hope. It is an entirely different way of thinking and talking from what I learned in my dysfunctional home, but it is a crucial way that we have learned to be family to one another. Some days the givens are hard to swallow, but they remind me of how far God has brought me, and my family, toward wholeness. They remind me that I am not bound by my past; in Christ I have hope for a future that looks entirely different from the past.

---

[1]Anne Wilson Schaef, *Codependence: Misunderstood—Mistreated* (San Francisco: Harper & Row, 1986), p. 21.

Study 1

Healing Dysfunctional Families

Joseph's life embodies so many admirable qualities—wisdom and foresight, just administration, leadership under adverse conditions, character forged through trial. His experience in Egypt encompassed times of privilege, times of persecution and imprisonment, and, finally, times of honor and power as ruler over all of Egypt. Through it all, he demonstrated both extraordinary ability and extraordinary integrity.

Yet Joseph's family was far from healthy. His father, Jacob, treated him with obvious favoritism over his brothers which resulted in a level of envy and malice that threatened Joseph's life. Joseph was the victim of his brothers' anger, but there is no evidence in his later life that he saw himself as a victim, powerless over his circumstances.

Joseph's story is a demonstration of God's sovereignty over the pain in our lives, and a model of how even the worst things that

happen to us can become opportunities for God to work out his
perfect will.

Read Genesis 37:1-11.
1. How did Jacob's treatment of Joseph result in an unhealthy situation in the family (vv. 3-4)? (Jacob is called *Israel* in verse 3. To
refresh your memory of Jacob's complex family, see Genesis 30.)

2. What evidence do you see that communication within the family
was not open and direct?

3. What were Joseph's dreams about (vv. 5-10)?

How did his presentation of the dreams further alienate him from
his brothers?

Read Genesis 37:12-36.
4. What is the result of the jealousy and alienation in Joseph's

family? Describe the impact on Joseph, his brothers and his father.

Genesis 39—41 describes Joseph's experiences in Potiphar's house, his imprisonment and his release after interpreting Pharaoh's dreams about the coming famine.

Read Genesis 42:1-24.
5. What do you think are the reasons Joseph doesn't identify himself to his brothers (v. 8)?

6. Verse 9 says, "He remembered his dreams about them." What do you think his dreams had to do with his actions here? (Refer back to Gen 37:5-10.)

7. Which aspects of the dreams are yet unfulfilled?

8. How does Joseph respond to his brothers' feelings of guilt (v. 24)?

Why doesn't Joseph show his tears (v. 24)?

Chapters 43 and 44 describe the brothers' second trip to Egypt, this time with Benjamin. Joseph gives them food, but sets a trap that makes Benjamin a slave. Judah, who has pledged his life as a guarantee of Benjamin's safety, pleads with Joseph to release the youngest brother. Finally, Joseph reveals his identity to them.

Read Genesis 45:1-11.
9. How does Joseph interpret his experiences to his brothers (vv. 5-11)?

10. How do God's blessings compare with the evil done to Joseph?

Read Genesis 50:15-22.
11. In what sense are the brothers still bound by their guilt, even

seventeen years after their reunion with Joseph?

How does Joseph respond to their pleas (vv. 19-21)?

12. *Response:* Think of any situations in your life that make you wonder what good God could possibly bring out of them. How does Joseph's story challenge or encourage you?

For Further Study: Genesis 30; 39-41; 43-44; 46-47.

Study 2

Healing Emotional Pain

Painful emotions are almost always part of the experience of growing up in a dysfunctional family. We have often been sinned against, victims of emotional, if not physical, abuse and neglect. These experiences hurt long after the fact.

Too often adults from dysfunctional families have never allowed themselves to experience the pain of their childhood. We might have much to grieve, but find ourselves reluctant to enter into the process of grieving. And in the present the vestiges of dysfunctional behavior can create stress and conflict in relationships, thus multiplying that pain and sorrow in our lives.

The good news for us is that God is a God of comfort. In sharing our human experiences, Jesus felt our pain. Our hope for healing lies in him.

Read Matthew 5:1-6.

1. What does it mean to be poor in spirit (v. 3)?

2. How would someone feeling painful emotions be spiritually poor?

3. What does the Lord promise to the poor in spirit?

What is the kingdom of heaven?

4. The word translated "blessed" in the beatitudes means "happy." How can mourning and happiness go together?

How can grief be a positive experience in your life?

5. What is the promise to those who mourn (v. 4)?

How does that make you feel?

6. Hunger and thirst can be painful experiences. How can a person's desire for righteousness be compared with physical hunger and thirst?

7. How is righteousness related to emotional wholeness?

8. Jesus' promise is that those who desire righteousness will be filled. What would that fulfillment look like for you?

9. How do the beatitudes contrast with our usual ideas about emotions, especially negative ones?

Read 2 Corinthians 1:3-11.
10. What promise do you find in these verses?

11. How do these verses help you to understand why Christians suffer from pain, illness and death when God could certainly deliver or heal them every time?

12. What role do the prayers of other believers play in your experiences of hardship and sorrow?

13. *Response:* Commit yourself to being vulnerable with other Christians in order to receive the comfort God offers through the body of Christ.

For Further Study: Proverbs 7:22; Psalm 34:18.

Study 3

Dealing with Anger

Anger is an emotion common to all people, but those of us who grew up in dysfunctional families tend to have particular difficulty handling our anger. Our anger is often tied to the hurts of the past, and our reaction to feeling insecure can be lashing out with angry words or even actions. Anger nursed and remembered over long periods of time can turn into bitterness, a root that inevitably takes on a life of its own and blossoms in destructive attitudes and behaviors.

Anger in itself is not sin. It is simply an emotion, a God-given part of life as a human being. It's a natural reaction to threats or injuries; yet anger is all too often expressed in ways that spread the harm around.

The Old Testament is full of references to God's righteous anger or indignation against sin, and this emotional aspect of God's character also appears in the New Testament through Christ. How can we learn to "be angry, but sin not"?

Read Mark 3:1-6.
1. Why is Jesus angry (v. 5)?

Why was Jesus "deeply distressed" at the same time he was angry?

2. How does Jesus respond out of this mixture of emotions?

Read Psalm 4.
3. What is David angry about (v. 2)?

4. How does David deal with his anger (vv. 1, 3)?

5. In verse 4 David suggests that we can be angry and not sin. How do you think that could be possible?

6. What do you think David means by the phrase "search your hearts and be silent" (v. 4)?

How can reflecting on angry feelings be a healthy way of dealing with anger?

Read Ephesians 4:25-32.
7. What is the relationship between letting the sun go down on your anger and giving the devil a foothold (vv. 26-27)?

8. How does this help you to understand how we are to practice the instruction "in your anger do not sin" (v. 26)?

Compare Ephesians 4:29 with Proverbs 15:1.
9. What negative effects can our words have on others?

How can words be used to build people up instead of tearing them down?

10. In Ephesians 4:31 we are told to "get rid of all bitterness, rage and anger." Sometimes, however, we don't recognize these emotions in ourselves. What evidences of unrecognized anger could you look for in your behavior, words or attitudes?

11. In verse 32, Paul mentions some positive attitudes that Christians should have in contrast to anger. What are they?

How can these attitudes help you deal with anger in less destructive ways?

12. *Response:* Which area of your life gives you the most trouble in handling anger (for example, job, school, family, friendships)?

What steps can you take to deal with anger in more appropriate ways?

For Further Study: Proverbs 22:24-25; James 1:19-20.

Study 4

The Power of Forgiveness

Christians *are forgiven people, but forgiving others can still be one* of the hardest things we have to do. It is a distinctly unnatural act to put aside defensiveness, hurt, anger and blame in order to forgive and seek forgiveness.

Unreconciled relationships are continuing sources of pain to us. They are wounds in our hearts, no matter who we believe was originally at fault. They hamper our testimony to the world. Jesus said, "They will know you are my disciples by your love." Therefore, what does our lack of love say?

Ultimately, our broken relationships get in the way of our relationship with God. We are told to be reconciled with our brothers and sisters in Christ before we enter into God's presence (Mt 5:24-25).

Read Matthew 18:15-35.
1. What guidelines does Jesus put forth for reconciling a relationship

with someone who has offended you (vv. 15-17)?

2. What are some reasons for approaching the offending person privately and directly?

3. What should your motivation be in approaching someone in this way?

4. What do you think is the purpose of Peter's question in verse 21?

5. The servant in the parable owed the equivalent of several million dollars, yet he refused to forgive a debt of only a few dollars (vv. 24-27). How would you compare what you "owed" God and what another person might owe you?

6. How does the parable of the unmerciful servant add to our understanding of the instructions Jesus gave for dealing with conflict in relationships?

Read Luke 6:27-36.
7. Why do you think we are instructed to respond to our enemies, or those who treat us badly, with love?

8. What reward does Jesus promise for those who show love in these difficult circumstances (v. 35)?

9. Why is mercy the aspect of God's character are we encouraged to imitate (v. 36)?

Read Colossians 3:12-14.
10. What do you think the qualities listed in verse 12 have to do with

the instruction to forgive in verse 13?

11. The words *clothe youselves* imply a command; in what sense do you see taking on these qualities as an act of the will?

12. What does it mean to forgive "as God forgave" us? Describe the nature of God's forgiveness of our sins.

13. *Response:* Who do you need to forgive or seek forgiveness of?

How will you begin to reconcile that relationship? (If you are studying this guide with a group, can the members of the group encourage you or hold you accountable?)

Study 5

Understanding Guilt

Conviction *of sin is a necessary part of any recovery—without it we* are not aware of our need for God and would never turn to him in faith. But frequently the guilt we feel is something else: another person's manipulation or the result of an overdeveloped sense of responsibility for everything inside and outside of us. False or unearned guilt negates the forgiveness we have received in Jesus Christ.

Guilty feelings make us run for cover, like Adam and Eve hiding in the garden. Denial or self-deception is a common response of people from dysfunctional backgrounds to feelings such as guilt, anger and pain. We would rather pretend that these feelings and the relationships and memories behind them aren't real than face up to the consequences.

Into this cycle of injury, pain, guilt and denial Jesus interjects radical words, "You will know the truth, and the truth will set you free" (Jn 8:32). Accepting reality and facing the truth is the first step toward freedom and a new way of life.

Read Psalm 32:1-7.
1. Describe the suffering produced by the guilt of unconfessed sin (vv. 3-4).

2. How do guilt feelings permeate all that we experience?

3. What changes can you see in the author after he confesses his sin (vv. 6-7)?

Read John 13:1-11.
4. How does Peter react to the idea that Jesus wants to wash his feet (v. 8)?

5. Why does Peter think he needs to be washed all over (v. 9)?

6. What is Jesus saying about sin and grace in verse 10?

7. What was wrong with Peter's view of himself?

8. How is false guilt a denial of Christ?

Read 1 John 3:16-20.
9. How can you know the difference between true guilt (conviction of sin) and false guilt (vv. 19-20)?

10. What promise do you find here to help you deal with false guilt?

11. *Response:* Begin to walk in the light, and not in darkness, by considering what loving "with actions and in truth" (v. 18) means to you.

For Further Study: 1 John 1:1-10.

Study 6

Finding Your Identity in God

Children *growing up in dysfunctional families are not given accurate* reflections of themselves and their worth. Low self-esteem can be a crippling result of such an upbringing, but so can an idea of personal worth that is based on achievements or the approval of others. A person who does not feel secure about his or her own worth is likely to find unhealthy ways of bolstering self-worth—by becoming a slave to others' expectations or by cutting others down to size.

The Bible says that all people are ultimately worthy: Human dignity rests on the fact that we are all created in God's image. To base our self-worth on anything else is to build our lives on very shaky ground. The fact that God accepts us, as unworthy and messed-up as our lives might be, is the only good reason for accepting ourselves. And acceptance is the beginning of change.

Read Psalm 139:1-16.

1. What are the implications of God's knowledge of your actions, thoughts and words (vv. 1-4)?

2. What does it mean that God has his hand upon you (v. 5)?

3. What image comes to mind as you read verse 10?

4. When did God's commitment to you as a person begin, according to this psalm (v. 13)?

How does that make you feel?

5. The psalmist's reaction to God's involvement in his formation and birth was praise. What specific things about your body, personality and spirit demonstrate the creative power of God?

6. What is your reaction to the psalmist's statement in verse 16 that all his days were ordained by God?

Read Romans 8:15-17.
7. What is the role of the Holy Spirit in confirming our identity as God's children (vv. 15-16)?

8. What do the facts that we call God *Father* and that we are "heirs of God" tell us about our value in God's eyes (v. 17)?

Read Romans 8:28-39.
9. Verses 28 and 29 tell us that God is working on our behalf in order to fulfill his purpose for us. What is that purpose?

10. What price did God pay on our behalf (vv. 32-34)?

11. What conclusions does Paul draw from God's commitment to us in Christ (v. 35)?

12. What reassurances do verses 35-39 give us in the midst of troubling circumstances?

13. *Response:* How do you need to modify your self-understanding to better reflect your knowledge of who you are in Christ Jesus?

How will changes in your self-understanding also change your actions?

For Further Study: John 10:28-29; James 1:22-25.

Suggestions for Leaders

Leading a Bible discussion can be an enjoyable and rewarding experience. But it can also be intimidating—especially if you've never done it before. If this is how you feel, you're in good company. When God asked Moses to lead the Israelites out of Egypt, he replied, "O Lord, please send someone else to do it!" (Ex 4:13). But God's response to all of his servants—including you—is essentially the same: "My grace is sufficient for you" (2 Cor 12:9).

There is another reason you should feel encouraged. Leading a Bible discussion is not difficult if you follow certain guidelines. You don't need to be an expert on the Bible or a trained teacher. The suggestions listed below should enable you to effectively and enjoyably fulfill your role as leader.

Preparing for the Study

1. Ask God to help you understand and apply the passage in your own life. Unless this happens, you will not be prepared to lead others. Pray too for the various members of the group. Ask God to open your hearts to the message of his Word and motivate you to action.

2. Read the introduction to the entire guide to get an overview of the subject at hand and the issues which will be explored. If you want to do more reading on the topic, check out the resource section at the end of the guide for appropriate books and magazines.

3. As you begin each study, read and reread the assigned Bible passages to familiarize yourself with them. Read the passages suggested for further study as well. This will give you a broader picture of how these issues are discussed throughout Scripture.

4. This study guide is based on the New International Version of the Bible. It will help you and the group if you use this translation as the basis for your study and discussion.

5. Carefully work through each question in the study. Spend time in meditation and reflection as you consider how to respond.

6. Write your thoughts and responses in the space provided in the study guide. This will help you to express your understanding of the passage clearly.

7. It might help you to have a Bible dictionary handy. Use it to look up any unfamiliar words, names or places. (For additional help on how to study a passage, see chapter five of *Leading Bible Discussions,* IVP.)

8. Take the response portion of each study seriously. Consider what this means for your life—what changes you might need to make in your lifestyle and/or actions you need to take in the world. Remember that the group will follow your lead in responding to the studies.

Leading the Study

1. Begin the study on time. Open with prayer, asking God to help the group to understand and apply the passage.

2. Be sure that everyone in your group has a study guide. Encourage the group to prepare beforehand for each discussion by reading the introduction to the guide and by working through the questions in the study.

3. At the beginning of your first time together, explain that these studies are meant to be discussions, not lectures. Encourage the members of the group to participate. However, do not put pressure on those who may be hesitant to speak during the first few sessions.

4. Have a group member read the introductory paragraph at the beginning of the discussion. This will orient the group to the topic of the study.

5. Have a group member read aloud the passage to be studied. (When there is more than one passage, the Scripture is divided up throughout the study so that you won't have to keep several passages in mind at the same time.)

6. As you ask the questions, keep in mind that they are designed to be used just as they are written. You may simply read them aloud. Or you may prefer to express them in your own words. There may be times when it is appropriate to deviate from the study guide. For example, a question may have already been answered. If so, move on to the next question. Or someone may raise an important question not covered in the guide. Take time to discuss it, but try to keep the group from going off on tangents.

7. Avoid answering your own questions. If necessary, repeat or rephrase them until they are clearly understood. An eager group quickly becomes passive and silent if they think the leader will do most of the talking.

8. Don't be afraid of silence. People may need time to think about the question before formulating their answers.

9. Don't be content with just one answer. Ask, "What do the rest of you think?" or "Anything else?" until several people have given answers to the question.

10. Acknowledge all contributions. Try to be affirming whenever possible. Never reject an answer. If it is clearly off-base, ask, "Which verse led you to that conclusion?" or again, "What do the rest of you think?"

11. Don't expect every answer to be addressed to you, even though this will probably happen at first. As group members become more at ease, they will begin to truly interact with each other. This is one sign of healthy discussion.

12. Don't be afraid of controversy. It can be very stimulating. If you don't resolve an issue completely, don't be frustrated. Move on and keep it in mind for later. A subsequent study may solve the problem.

13. Periodically summarize what the group has said about the passage. This helps to draw together the various ideas mentioned and gives continuity to the study. But don't preach.

14. Don't skip over the response question. Be willing to get things started by describing how you have been convicted by the study and what action you'd like to take. Consider doing a service project as a group in response to what you're learning from the studies. Alternately, hold one another accountable to get involved in some kind of active service.

15. Conclude your time together with conversational prayer. Ask for God's help in following through on the commitments you've made.

16. End on time.

Many more suggestions and helps are found in *The Small Group Leader's Handbook* and *Good Things Come in Small Groups* (both from IVP). Reading through one of these books would be worth your time.

Resources

Publications

Beattie, Melody. *Codependent No More.* San Francisco: Harper & Row, 1987.

Beattie, Melody. *Beyond Codependency and Getting Better All the Time.* San Francisco: Harper & Row, 1989.

Carlson, Dwight. *Overcoming Hurts and Anger.* Eugene, Oreg.: Harvest House, 1981.

Harrison, Dan. *Strongest in the Broken Places: A Story of Spiritual Recovery.* Downers Grove, Ill.: InterVarsity Press, 1990.

Mellody, Pia; Miller, Andrea Wells; and Miller, J. Keith. *Facing Codependence.* San Francisco: Harper & Row, 1989.

Ryan, Dale and Juanita. *Recovery from Family Dysfunctions.* Life Recovery Guides. Downers Grove, Ill.: InterVarsity Press, 1990.

Seamands, David A. *Healing for Damaged Emotions.* Wheaton, Ill.: Victor, 1981.

Seamands, David A. *Putting Away Childish Things.* Wheaton, Ill.: Victor, 1984.

Seamands, David A. *Healing Grace.* Wheaton, Ill.: Victor, 1988.

Schaef, Anne Wilson. *Co-dependence: Misunderstood—Mistreated.* San Francisco: Harper & Row, 1986.

Thompson, Bruce, and Barbara Thompson. *Walls of My Heart.* Euclid, Minn.: Crown Ministries International, 1989.

The Twelve Steps and Twelve Traditions. New York: Alcoholics Anonymous World Service.

The Twelve Steps—A Spiritual Journey. San Diego, Calif.: Recovery Publications, 1988.

Whitfield, Charles L. *Healing the Child Within.* Deerfield Beach, Fla.: Health Communications, 1987.

Wilson, Sandra. *Released from Shame.* Downers Grove, Ill.: InterVarsity Press, 1990.

Organizations

Please note that there are many other twelve-step groups that are geared for specific types of addiction or compulsive behavior. These organizations can put you in touch with groups in your area.

Adult Children of Alcoholics, Central Service Board, P.O. Box 3216, Torrance, Calif. 90505; (213) 534-1815.

Co-dependents Anonymous, P.O. Box 33577, Phoenix, Ariz. 85067-3577; (602) 944-0141.

Overcomers Outreach, 2290 West Whittier Blvd., La Habra, Calif. 90631; (213) 697-3994.

Appendix

The Twelve Steps and Related Scripture[1]

Step One
We admitted we were powerless over our separation from God—that our lives had become unmanageable.
I know nothing good lives in me, that is, in my sinful nature. For I have the desire to do what is good, but I cannot carry it out. (Romans 7:18)

Step Two
Came to believe that a power greater than ourselves could restore us to sanity.
For it is God who works in you to will and to act according to his good purpose. (Philippians 2:13)

Step Three
Made a decision to turn our will and our lives over to the care of God as we understood Him.
Therefore, I urge you, brothers, in view of God's mercy, to offer your bodies as living sacrifices, holy and pleasing to God—which is your spiritual worship. (Romans 12:1)

Step Four
Made a searching and fearless moral inventory of ourselves.
Let us examine our ways and test them, and let us return to the Lord. (Lamentations 3:40)

Step Five
Admitted to God, to ourselves, and to another human being the exact nature of our wrongs.
Therefore confess your sins to each other and pray for each other so that you may be healed. (James 5:16a)

Step Six
Were entirely ready to have God remove all these defects of character.
Humble yourselves before the Lord, and he will lift you up. (James 4:10)

Step Seven
Humbly asked Him to remove our shortcomings.
If we confess our sins, he is faithful and just and will forgive us our sins and purify us from all unrighteousness. (1 John 1:9)

Step Eight
Made a list of all persons we had harmed and became willing to make amends to them all.
Do to others as you would have them do to you. (Luke 6:31)
Step Nine
Made direct amends to such people wherever possible, except when to do so would injure them or others.
Therefore, if you are offering your gift at the altar and there remember that your brother has something against you, leave your gift there in front of the altar. First go and be reconciled to your brother; then come and offer your gift. (Matthew 5:23-24)
Step Ten
Continued to take personal inventory and, when we were wrong, promptly admitted it.
So, if you think you are standing firm, be careful that you don't fall. (1 Corinthians 10:12)
Step Eleven
Sought through prayer and meditation to improve our conscious contact with God as we understood Him, praying only for knowledge of His will for us and the power to carry that out.
Let the word of Christ dwell in you richly. (Colossians. 3:16a)
Step Twelve
Having had a spiritual awakening as the result of these steps, we tried to carry this message to others, and to practice these principles in all our affairs.
Brothers, if someone is caught in a sin, you who are spiritual should restore him gently. But watch yourself, or you also may be tempted. (Galatians 6:1)

¹Taken from *The Twelve Steps—A Spiritual Journey*. San Diego, Calif.: Recovery Publications, 1988. Used by permission.